Whisperings of Self

Whisperings of Self

by Validivar

*A collection of aphorisms designed to uplift
and inspire each day of the year*

ROSICRUCIAN LIBRARY
VOLUME XXIX

Supreme Grand Lodge of AMORC, Inc.
Printing and Publishing Department
San Jose, California

First Edition, 1969
Sixth Edition, 1986
Copyright 1969, 1978, and 1986
by Supreme Grand Lodge of AMORC, Inc.
All Rights Reserved

Library of Congress Catalog Card No.: 68-57028

ISBN 0-912057-40-8

Second Printing 1978
Third Printing 1981
Fourth Printing 1986
Fifth Printing 1989

Printed and Bound in U.S.A.

Our friends are selected by the virtues which we attribute to them. In such persons we see *loyalty, understanding, dependability*, and *camaraderie*. To them from whom I have derived encouragement and inspiration I have dedicated this book.

VALIDIVAR

The Rosicrucian Library

Volume

(Other volumes will be added from time to time.
Write for complete catalog.)

Preface

Whisperings of Self is a collection of intuitive impressions received by a great mystic philosopher, Ralph M. Lewis, who in this work writes under the pen name of Validivar.

Known to Rosicrucians throughout the world as the head of that renowned mystic fraternity, Ralph Lewis has also received acclaim in the literary world as an author of books and articles on psychology, mysticism, metaphysics, and philosophy.

The aphorisms in this collection have appeared singly in copies of the *Rosicrucian Digest* over a period of forty years, and comprise insights into all areas of human experience—justice, war and peace, ethics, morals, marriage, family, work, leisure, and countless others.

The words chosen succinctly describe the pattern of the universe. They tell of the hows, whens, wheres, and whys of existence. More than that, they serve as guides to show man the way to fulfillment— as guardians to ward off the ills that might beset him.

Ralph Lewis' frank and direct style provides much food for thought in each brief impression. A reader develops the habit of using a thought for a day, and there are more than two hundred from which to choose.

These are truly personal guides to daily living, and we hope that they will serve you well.

Arthur C. Piepenbrink

The moral motivation for goodness on the part of man is both biological and psychological. It is the desire for the harmony of one's own being with his surroundings.

Study is the conscious effort to learn; the pleasure to be gained is a secondary motive.

There can never be a paradise populated with men of low intent and little restraint.

Any condition that always occurs in relation to a phenomenon is a law.

We are rich only when we do not want more than we have, regardless of how little that may be.

A thing has intrinsic value if its essence is in demand because of its essential contribution to some human purpose.

The strong are those who show compassion for the weak, for they are able to resist the vanity of their strength.

Tolerance is an attitude which preserves individualism without jeopardizing the welfare of a whole people.

We live by what we know not by what may be so.

The past is an image of what men once thought and did. It becomes an incentive to try and emulate it or rise above it.

Tolerance is the recognition of the right of others to any actions or expressions of thought which are not contrary to what a *whole people* conceive as their welfare.

Public decency is the attempt to preserve that evolved aspect of self to which man has laboriously attained.

Homely philosophy is an appeal to popular opinion rather than a challenge to individual reason.

Never hire a friend, but be friendly to those you hire.

The human's five senses are the result of his organic dependence upon those characteristics of reality we call *motion, mass,* and *attraction.*

A virtue is a self-disciplinary action by which a certain standard of behavior is attained.

Frustration arises from infringement of unrelated ideas upon one another preventing the satisfactory culmination of any single one.

Superstitions are the assumption of causes. They are substitutes for unknown causes or the attempt to invoke those that do not exist.

When writing or speaking, be informative. No one likes to chew on chaff.

Rosicrucianism is not a particular subject but rather the furtherance of the spirit and application of knowledge.

Whisperings of Self

If solely by his own reasoning one can arrive at the same conclusions as the great thinkers before him, he should find encouragement in his pursuits; for it is only the limits of his own mind which may prevent him from surpassing them. No man is inherently great. It is only the exercise of those powers which are his that makes him so. A Socrates and an Aristotle were not destined to be; they became such.

Reason is a blade that grows dull if not whetted with thought.

The ideal of the true society must be to so monitor the powers and faculties of men that each may realize the wholeness of his being.

The good in life should be a human creation in relation to events, not a search for a latent, inherent good in nature or the world.

If philosophy is the love of wisdom, then science is the love of coherence.

It is better to think and occasionally be found wrong than to be always right because you are a follower of another.

Human relations is the study of mankind with the purpose of revealing and removing the basic causes of conflict among men.

The inconsistency of the television audience is that it finds satisfaction for hours in idly watching a portrayal of the *active* lives of others.

Inferiority is not a virtue by which all that exceeds it is to be protested as a vice.

14

Perhaps most of our dissatisfaction with life comes from the fact that our pursuits of happiness are too numerous. Each thing sought in itself seems crystal clear in the joy it will afford. But collectively, they detract from each other and diminish our enthusiasm for any one of them like an assortment of art treasures heaped high.

A life is lived in a moment of ecstasy.

No man is free whose mind is not like a door with a double-acting hinge swinging outward to release his own ideas and inward to receive the worthy thoughts of others.

The challenge to almost all philosophers has been: We are and the world appears to be, yet if one alone is real, why the other? If both are real, how may they be conceived as one?

In general, God is the ultimate of the individual's conception of supreme power, initial cause, and moral perfection.

In general, God is the ultimate of the individual's conception of supreme power, initial cause, and moral perfection.

☾

A miracle is a perceived effect of an unperceived cause.

☾

If we know all there is and the laws thereof, there is still the mystery of the cause.

☾

Human progress continues only so long as the human concept can exceed attainment.

☾

The struggle for freedom is the primitive and eternal fight of human will against necessity, natural and social, which imposes itself upon man.

Whisperings of Self

The higher form of society, which we call civilization, really begins with a growing self-consciousness and the attempt to have it discipline the whole of human behavior.

The vocative and written word can be dynamic. It is a force, once released, not easily controlled. Therefore, nothing should be more carefully selected than our words.

The greatest thoughts are simply expressed, for their simplicity is evidence of their clarity.

Good is the content of whatever men call happiness.

Something can only be an ideal by comparison with something else whose context stands as inferior.

Arrogance is an increased consciousness of power accompanied by a decreased conscience.

What have we learned from war? How to fear the next one even more!

The principal human fault which gives rise to evil is to see things outside their true relationship.

Reason as knowledge excels perception because it always concerns itself with first principles, causes— either of the past or the future. Perception is limited to effects, no matter how causal they may appear to be.

Rights are privileges which men grant each other in mutual respect of human dignity.

Perfect knowledge is that which for the moment is irrefutable by anyone and about which you entertain no doubt.

In their relations in the state, men should be honest, not alone because of moral edict but because, if they are not, they strike at the existence of society upon which they depend for greater personal expression.

Suspicion is an intangible but nefarious film that insulates human minds one from the other.

There are no personal ends in life that can exceed health of the body and peace of mind for the self.

It is not death but a forceful separation from life that most men fear.

Most of the particulars or ends which men pursue in life in the hope of finding peace of mind, though often by some other term, actually impede or destroy their own capacity to attain peace.

The law of self-preservation is the excercise of self—the furtherance of self in all of its aspects. If we did not further self, there would be no further self.

A thing does not exist unless it has meaning, for identity depends upon the significance of experience. The understanding derived from experience corresponds to reality.

Anyone who recommends giving up intellectual, cultural, or spiritual ground gained because it is hoary with age is bereft or reason.

Science began when man no longer presumed to know the connections between objects but first had to demonstrate their existence objectively.

A mission in life is a purpose toward which the individual conceives that all his powers and functions should be directed.

One awakens the soul not by being ignorant of evil but only by calling on his inner qualities to sustain him from known temptations.

Referring to destruction in nature is man's way of saying that nature has opposed his sense of values.

The thinker is the one who uses what he collects in the way of experience.

There is a kind of general goodness which seems to youth to exist in the newness of all experience. Therefore, youth can afford to expend itself, to take chances, to make mistakes because of the resiliency of its spirit.

True education is the intentional acquisition of knowledge through guided experience. It has as its objective not just the development of a particular skill but, as well, the cultivation of the mental faculties. By means of it, one comes to exercise his creative powers thereby preserving his intellectual freedom and individuality.

There is no wound so severe as that of a ruptured ego, and none that heals more slowly.

It's not the quantity but the quality of reading that stimulates thought.

The most discouraging thing in life is the approach toward the unfinished end. This, perhaps more than any other thing, prompts the hope in a hereafter or future life.

Man is not by Cosmic intent but by Cosmic necessity; within the necessity of the Cosmic's nature there arise such complexities, of which man is one.

An intuitive truth is one that satisfies the emotional as well as the reasoning self. Intuitive truths are those which are simply arrived at and appear inspirational. Because they seem to flash into consciousness, rather than being arrived at, they allay suspicion that they may have suffered in the process of reasoning.

Knowing is realizing that a thing is, but *understanding* is knowing what that thing is.

Wisdom is the cultivating of the ability to discern the effects of applied knowledge. The wise man has been able to combine experience into a pattern of action whose effects are propitious.

In theory, conscience may be explained as the subconscious desire to live sympathetically and cooperatively with one's fellows. This is accomplished by establishing some ground, some behavior, to represent such feelings.

Figuratively, we may change the color of the glasses through which we peer out at Cosmic reality, but we will always be conferring an illusionary quality upon it as a result of such glasses.

The logical premise underlying any moral system should be *that which is best for the most*—at the time.

The most difficult art to cultivate: getting along with what you have.

●

The liberal mind is one that has not established an unwarranted allegiance to inherited and untried concepts.

●

There is no mystery greater than nature and no adventure greater than its solution.

●

In effect, law is the enforcement of a stipulated practice or principle which the governing power of society wishes to perpetuate.

●

An accident is a natural event that occurs without intent.

It is not true that just positive thought alone is power. All thought is power! It is the application of that power which we normally call positive or negative.

Nothing is God, and yet God is everything.

You can take everything away from a man but his thoughts.

Let us remember that prejudice is not the conclusion of reason, for it never offers a rational explanation for its objections.

A democratic nation is one in which individuals create a political instrument to preserve the just exercise of their separate powers.

One must not stop progress, but first it must be determined whether a change is progress.

☾

Man may be divine in essence, but he is still an animal in substance.

☾

How can a man who does not think be free? Only a thinker makes a true choice. All others are bound to the influence of suggestion, either subtle or direct.

☾

The only way to enjoy a rest is to work for it.

☾

It is far easier to arouse the ire of a man than to appeal to his reason. Until there is a transition in this condition of human nature, we may expect society to display passion more often than wisdom in attempting solutions to its problems.

27

The beautiful is that harmony of things and conditions which is pleasurable to one or more of the senses of man.

Continuity of space corresponds to continuity of duration in time. If space has existence that is infinite, then its duration, or time, is likewise infinite. Something cannot *be* without likewise being an *event*.

The spirit of nationalism is the spirit of security for the resources and interests of the group of which the individual is a part. It is loyalty to self-interest on a collective scale.

Human dignity is the particular status that mankind believes it has attained in its physical, mental, and moral development. To retain this dignity requires self-discipline.

In the mysteries of the universe are the glories men attribute to their gods.

Mysticism is an inner conviction born of subtle feeling.

The behavior of conscience, the form which it objectively assumes, is the result of experience in human relations, customs, and inherited traditions.

Those who live should ask themselves: "What are you doing here?" Within their answer will be bared their whole philosophy of life.

The best of tradition is, after all, but static, an intermediate resting place between a lesser state and one yet to be attained.

He who entertains a new avenue of thought is a metaphysician. He who demonstrates it is a scientist.

The only supreme right among men in society is the collective power they assign it by their unfettered wills, their own volition.

Strict conformity in society is basically repetitious conduct. It rarely contributes anything of importance to the culture of the period.

Philosophy is the organization of human experience so as to better serve the individual's life.

Destiny is a fabric of events woven on the loom of time.

Many an authoritative opinion is but an educated conjecture.

Why Time Seems Shorter With Age

In youth, the consciousness is crowded with many new experiences which hold the attention. The duration of the succession of experiences thus seems drawn out.

With age, many experiences each day and week have become repetitious. They have little demand upon our attention. The succession of experiences, therefore, seems less, and the duration or time shorter.

Only those who fear the truth lie.

There is nothing greater in life than a wholesome happiness, but it has to be created. It is not to be found, nor is it a caprice of the mere act of living.

31

It is always easier to coast than pull, but one is downhill; the other is the upward climb.

A truly progressive civilization is one that cultivates the character as well as the environment of man.

Doing anything in a habitual and ceremonial way that will perpetuate a desired ideal and emotional feeling is a ritual.

The greatest philosophers have recognized the relative value of the *scientific* approach to knowledge.

The greatest scientists have evolved a *philosophy* from their study of phenomena.

The greater the number of things one possesses, the greater is his responsibility for them.

Whisperings of Self

Considerable of today's crime is the result of the urge of the ego to cast aside the cloak of obscurity that has descended upon it. It is a negative struggle to prevent a submersion of the self.

Man is a dependent element of nature but independent as to his conception of her. His freedom, thus, lies solely in the view he chooses to take of this relationship.

The Earth is one great table at which we must all learn to sit and share its bounty. The world is too small to further divide among diversified political states.

Habits are born out of experience and tradition. Experience is a product of time and circumstance. What one period and event makes plausible or practical today may not be so tomorrow.

Responsibility is a *response* to a conceived value. This response is an obligation to preserve the value.

❂

Soul is our conception of the indwelling aspects of self. Personality is our expression of that conception in thought and deed.

❂

Many moral systems have inherited the obsolescence of the religion from which they emerged.

❂

The Cosmic is universal and infinite in its manifestation, but it is individual and finite in human experience and conception.

❂

Religion is a series of customs and beliefs intended to bring us into conformity with a supreme supernatural power.

Resistance makes persistance. The strength of will is in its power of opposition.

If a religion must control the political and physical force of the state to maintain its supremacy, it admits its lack of human appeal.

Will is in the mind's creation of a desire, a mental urge which motivates one to act in accordance with it.

True luxury is the extravagance of possessions.

Intuition consists of an unconscious reorganization of our existing ideas into an order of greater clarity.

Society must preserve the dignity of personal thought and action within the bounds of common security.

It is not that in which man immures his conception of God that matters, but what the ideal of God causes to occur within man.

Men are united by the fact of religious experience, not by their collective interpretation of it.

Each religion is a *mystical experience* had by its founder, out of which grows the creed it expounds.

Many men take an excursion from their faith only to return to it at the end of life like a weary traveler coming home.

Orthodoxy is an evil to be found alike in religion and science.

Practical Christian living is nothing more than the natural development of satisfactory human relations. This finds its equivalent in any highly developed moral order.

For most men, all human endeavor falls into three divisions: that which is commonplace and appears comprehensible; that which, like the sciences, is mysterious but by custom is acceptable; that which is mysterious but, being uncommon, is damned.

It can be positively declared that the decadence of a civilization begins when the effort to obtain the necessities of life is diminished to a minimum, and there is no corresponding effort to attain moral idealism.

The most golden treasures of life are its beautiful memories.

The labors involved in complex living are far in excess of the pleasures extracted therefrom.

Everything is both cause and effect. It is an *effect* of a past cause. But it is likewise a *cause* of the effect that will emerge from it in the future.

There is, therefore, neither an absolute cause nor effect. They both arise as a notion from our perception of any particular cycle of change.

Philosophy theorizes on the probable unity of the universe. *Science* tries to prove the existence of such unity by revealing interlocking laws and phenomena. *Mysticism*, however, provides the actual experience of unity through such states as Cosmic Consciousness.

No man can be honest in his convictions who has not first explored the possibility of an opposite view.

The fulfillment of desire creates obligation.

Consciousness is a state which an organism undergoes as the result of stimuli acting upon it. It may be likened to the motion of an object, which is a form of change through which the object passes as the result of forces acting upon it. Therefore, consciousness is neither a tangible nor intangible substance.

He who interrupts my thoughts, interrupts my life.

Each lends the color of his understanding to his surroundings.

To state the obvious is not a declaration of knowledge.

As science explains the nature of our existence, philosophy relates the purpose of that existence, and mysticism provides the spirit of it.

It is easier to discourse upon what man is *not* than on what he is. In all that he differs—that is not all that he is.

There is no more deadly venom than that which flows from the slanderous pen.

The isolationist is always one who is never conscious of his dependence upon others outside the narrow sphere in which he has placed himself.

Conscience, or the moral sense, is the way in which we regard the relation of self to our environment.

If good is a reality, it must be experienced. Therefore, no man sins who knows not the good, but every man sins who *refuses* to know the good. Thus, the greatest sin of all is *willful ignorance.*

If one pursues the knowledge that he loves, he makes love of knowledge his real end. One with such an end in view never intentionally misuses the power of his knowledge. It is the prudent use of knowledge that constitutes wisdom.

The mystic is most suited by his teachings and beliefs to contribute to the expansion of moral behavior. He causes his conduct to become a compulsion from *within*, a response to self, rather than a social or legal enforcement.

Most superstitions would pass if we took the trouble to find a reason for our beliefs.

The more man, through science, extends the physical universe, that is, reveals heretofore unrevealed reality, the more he comes to realize that he must alter his concepts of the relationship of divinity to matter.

What is commonly known as moral behavior is the human attempt to pursue such a course of mental and physical conduct as will induce or arouse feeling sympathetic to the realization had of the Inner Self.

The pseudo-mystic smirks at other men's struggles with the problems of existence, while he retires into a self-created atmosphere of smug sanctity. He implies that neglect of the world means spiritual supremacy.

All men have the same destination in life—happiness. But there is no agreement on the road to take to it.

Aspiration is the desire to attain what the mind conceives would be the most satisfying experience!

Each man should so live that he is worthy of life and his work worthy of him.

It is far easier to resort to the pages of a book than to ideas of the mind. Consequently, there are more readers than thinkers.

The human consciousness is "the organizer of the universe." That aspect of being which is comprehensible to the mind appears as order.

The moral structure is but *one* fabric. Any contamination of it makes the whole imperfect. He who lies is also a thief, for has he not stolen another's trust in his words?

Prejudice: a dislike without reasonable provocation.

One should be neither elated nor grieved over the present. The present is so fleeting that the causes of either sentiment are past when their effects are realized. Therefore, just say of what you experience, "It is well."

If a thing is neither good nor bad, it is devoid of inherent purpose. The effects that follow from it are by necessity and not by intent.

Nature is neither good nor bad. The good of living, therefore, consists in adapting ourselves to those effects we prefer.

Moral perfection in its highest state is the ultimate equivalence of *personality and soul*.

The right is only such if it provides justice.

The more money a man has, the more he has to find a usefulness for; since most men are selfish, it soon satisfies their elemental wants. Then comes the disquieting realization that the only lasting happiness money provides is in spending it on others.

Happiness is hard to acquire and easy to lose if it consists of many things.

A peaceful life is the intelligent evaluation of what is good in existence and the obtaining of it, for that brings satisfaction as lasting as our days.

The essence of good speaking: Have something to say, and say it.

Every incident should be worthy of the moment in which it exists.

The recitation of a confession is the recitation of a lesson learned.

Most men take a problem, not to themselves, not into the chambers of their own minds, but to the first directory of persons whom they can consult.

Happiness is an extract from the compound of living, but the compound is an intelligent formula of ordered thinking and doing. It is not a chance combination of events.

Many men and women live so unintelligently and with such abandon that they are forever contracting mental and physical pains, which eventually cause them to see the end of life and happiness as nothing more or less than a freedom from their particular distemper.

❍

To do an honest work well is to earn a satisfaction.

❍

A fool's paradise is one in which peace rests upon ignorance of the future moment.

❍

The real value of self-assurance is the spirit of determination it arouses.

❍

Something which has merit only because it stands alone has no merit at all when with other things.

47

Radicalism is an oblique departure from a line of thought or action. Radicalism is dynamic and opportunistic. It forcefully grasps at the immediate time and circumstances to gain its objective. Radicalism is not tolerant of obstructive ideas. The intent of true radicalism is constructive even though revolutionary in its nature.

That which all men need is no man's property.

The only value of tradition to society is that it affords a platform to stand upon while reaching for something higher. If it becomes a weight which prevents the individual from rising, it has outlived its usefulness.

Take away my reason for living and you may as well take my life, for the latter is worthless without the former.

It's not how long you live but the satisfaction you derive from life that makes it worthwhile.

Moral discernment is instinctively relating to ourselves the results of our contemplated acts toward others.

The greatest illusion of existence is the attempt to explain it.

Each people finds a kind of spiritual satisfaction in the behavior they have been conditioned to accept. This becomes their moral values.

The mystery of the Absolute: No man knows it, nor will ever know it, but illumination comes to those who seek to know it.

If we refute all our illusions, there remains no world in which to exist.

What men term freedom is the right of one man to exercise his will as against another.

What you think constitutes happiness can be the cause of unhappiness.

The objective expression of morality represents the diversity of human intellect and experience.

Belief is a conclusion without the verification of experience. In the absence of any knowledge contrary to them, beliefs are the most positive factors of our thinking, for they represent the sum of our reasoning.

Faith is reliance upon the *implied* quality of things and conditions.

Cosmic Consciousness is the consciousness of spiritual causes as distinguished from the consciousness of phenomenal effects.

No matter what else, we can be daily grateful we have been put in touch with knowledge, for its source is inexhaustible.

A proof of character is humility when confronted with praise.

We are rich in worldly attainments and poor in inner comprehension and self-discipline. This kind of economy makes for moral bankruptcy.

Matter moves man, but it does so without volition, for there is no will in matter. The movement of matter is only by the necessity of its nature. Therefore, the elements of matter should not be the master of man.

Prejudice is the poisoner of reason and the assassinator of justice.

Consciousness is the motion of the force of life as form is the motion of matter.

Resoluteness without reason is folly.

Faith is a presumption of the nature of something. It is the unquestioned acceptance of appearances of things, whether words or objects.

Worthy accomplishments can provide memory with a pleasure that counters the lessening satisfaction of age.

Philosophy is an intelligent approach to life.

Thought is an act of volition; it is the deliberate forming of ideas. Whereas instinct drives, thought selects.

To live is no unique state, nor is it a particular credit to man. However, to make life a radiance that illuminates the human understanding is most worthy of man.

Human nature, like fruit, is ripened by time. Only then is its true flavor apparent.

Wisdom is the possession of no man, yet it can be had by all men.

Starved thought is often found in an overfed body.

Behind every purpose is the assumed need for a physical or mental or emotional satisfaction that was thought to be had by a certain pursuit, as a form of action.

Procrastination is a disease of the will.

It is the duty of the philosopher to speculate on possibilities which are not yet confirmable by science. The philosopher is to conceive channels of investigation and observation, the direction of which science shall take.

The emotions are what give value to life. Reason and judgment help in deciding the value.

○

Man pays homage to his god not in numbers of his kind but in the perfection of the individual.

○

No god is false if it be the product of a free conscience and spiritual impulse.

○

Space is perception without form.
Extension is the extent of the character of substance and of space.
Time is the duration of the period of consciousness.

○

Find some degree of happiness each day, for life gives no assurance that it may be attained at a future time.

Clock and Time

Even if we know how the clock works, have a mastery of its mechanism, why does it *do so?* In the case of the clock there is purpose; the *why* is to tell time. Assuming that the universe is not purposeful and man only is, then it is philosophy and idealism that must provide the *why*, the *purpose*. Can a mechanism be appreciated without a purpose?

The test of intelligence is a crisis.

The importance of a behavioral code as a life value is the conscious direction in life it provides man. It makes man not a fatalist, but rather a potential master of his fate.

Everyone has character—it constitutes the sum total of our volitional behavior under all circumstances and to the demands which are made upon us.

We do not believe we *are* because it sounds plausible that we are, or because someone gives us a reason for self. We conceive self, the ego, because of certain irrefutable impressions we have.

The care for things of pleasure can become a burden.

To mean something to somebody is one of the greatest satisfactions in life.

Happiness is not an ingredient of the Cosmic substance. It is a state of mind arising from the conscious adjustment each makes to the reality of his personal existence.

The Divine is realized through the ever-changing mentality and consciousness of man.

The mystic never departs from his intimate experience. It is part of his being. *He alone* must evaluate it.

Nature will remain chaotic to us if we do nothing but create a series of little circles around certain groups of laws.

Whoever copies, always follows.

The mystical consciousness permits us to be completely immersed periodically in the sea of infinity instead of just wading in it objectively as most of us do.

To *know* is to form a thought image about an experience; it is to establish an understanding of what is realized in consciousness.

The more dominant emotional and psychic attributes of the person constitute the structure of his personality.

We do not always *have* to do what we like to do, but we should try to *like* what we have to do.

What the mind conceives, man will eventually achieve.

The will always seeks good—it is the desire for a particular satisfaction. That to man is *good,* of a kind.

Men have tried so hard to know what cannot be known and, in doing so, have discovered what can be known.

Educated men must be more than textbooks, or computers, or single volumes of knowledge. They must, in all their learning, think of themselves as being an integrated part of mankind. Their knowledge and personal success must contribute to society.

Business can be corrupt not because it is business but because of the ethics in its application—or the lack of same brought to bear in connection with it.

Let us remember that he who lives best is he who lives wisely, for the years increase his happiness as they decrease his powers of physical and material accomplishments.

Choice is selection according to preference. We never choose against our own nature physically, intellectually, or emotionally. Consequently, how free is our choice?

Whisperings of Self

Abstract thought provides knowledge beyond the scope of objective experience.

To one who sees clearly the shadows of the past and the substance of the present, the future is not concealed.

The depth of feeling of spirituality is amorphous. No one's image of its source, no matter how refined and universally recognized, is its true and absolute nature.

True knowledge is the final judgment of experience.

Keep your own counsel. If freely offered it may fall on deaf ears and closed minds. Your experience and judgment have greater value when asked for.

The nature of self is only mysterious to the extent that our ignorance of its full capabilities makes it so.

Indecency in connection with sex can only be a retrogression from whatever standard of moral restraint has first been associated with it.

Tolerance is the extending to others the rights you demand for yourself.

Civilization is a complex of things and conditions created by man to provide for his physical demands and to express his preferred mental and emotional states.

To be brave one must have first feared, for bravery is the mastery of fear.

The love of life should not be in terms of profligacy but in the excellence of its development and expression.

How ignorant is he who knows all but not himself.

Men show concern for health when it fails them; when it serves them, they neglect it.

In predicting a future, man reveals his concept of the present. He sees in the future the fulfillment of ideals that transcend prevailing limitations, or calamitous effects that follow from faulty natural or human causes.

Generosity is a sharing of pleasure. But real charity is always accompanied by a willing sacrifice.

Mystically, unity is a more lofty attainment than is oneness. Oneness is that which exists within itself. There is therefore no striving to be, whereas in unity there is the motivation to enter into a greater relationship than the singleness of one's own being.

What are the fears of death? Are they the loss of loves, family, friends, possessions, and fame, or of an unknown crammed with the varieties of uncertainty extolled by religion and philosophy? Only the living can grieve, for in death there is naught to sorrow about.

An admission of ignorance is the first step toward acquiring knowledge.

The person who puts rational restraint upon his acts with relation to other humans is ultimately protecting his own rights and expression of self.

Being a free thinker does not mean being a mental rambler.

Perception provides through experience the fundamental substance of thought; reason and imagination compound them into an infinity of ideas.

Education does not necessarily make for profundity of thought. Intelligence, observation, meditation, and reason do.

It is knowledge that points what we do not know.

An actor in a role can change in appearance and mannerism. However, he has not changed his consciousness of self. A thousand persons may look alike but each realizes their difference.

The world is as good as man sees it and goodness is only as man values it.

If there is no God image which is acceptable to all men alike, then no man's image of God is wrong.

Fate is but a combination of circumstances, the natural causes of which are unknown to man.

Where one works exclusively for self-interest, he cannot by so doing avoid working *against* the necessary interests of others.

As an organ the stomach is relatively large but its capacity is finite; the mind is relatively small but its capacity is infinite: Thus we may overeat but never overthink.

There is nothing which can exist outside of that which is, and whatever is is part of the *all* that is.

What is man, without knowing what he is— nothing.

There is more to life than told in the pages of books.

Life is the Great Initiation—a crossing of the threshold from non-existence to self-realization. Its rites consist of the vicissitudes of life, each with its symbolic value. Ultimate attainment is the integrating of the total experience into an order of personal understanding and meaning.

What will money buy when it has destroyed all things of worth in obtaining it?

67

To youth is the future; to age is the fruit of experience.

Tolerance is recognizing the right of others to a difference of expression.

A thing cannot be considered as other than perfect in itself if there is nothing else by which it can be compared.

There is a cosmic economy which permits no waste of creation. Each phenomenon of nature has a relationship to all others. So too, there must be an economy of mankind.

Order is but an accepted persistence of an act or arrangement.

The mystical experience provides the pulse of the Absolute, if not its anatomy.

Familiarity may not breed contempt, but your worthy thoughts and actions are assured a greater recognition by those of a less close association.

There is a parallel *infinity* between vastness and minuteness. Reduction results in a seeming nothing, but such is of the same *infinity* as vastness. Since there is no permanency of form, the ultimate of evolution or devolution is *infinity*.

Do not let fantasy cloak your reason! Let fantasy be a creative process of the imagination grounded in the fabric of reason. Let it be a reaching out for demonstrable truth. Fantasy can soar, and it should, but never in so free a flight of the imagination that it loses contact with the fundamental laws of nature.

The inevitability of time: it quickens the attributes of youth and dulls the faculties of the aged.

It is not what a thing may be but what man may understand it to be that is the truth to him.

A true humanitarian is one that has so lived that he has brought happiness to others by his presence, by the very fact of his existence, and by the dignity his way of life has conferred upon mankind.

We must crusade against traditional darkness. Let us give mental and active support, legally and ethically, to all that which seeks to remove the screen that blinds man to the reality of the future. Let us analyze what we ordinarily and habitually accept as traditions and customs as to their true worth to mankind. What is worth enduring must not stand alone on its past but reveal as well an equal value to the future.

The *personal* attribute of life is *consciousness*. Without it, life is but a mechanistic process.

Who knows the first cause of all? We can only conceive it as we feel it.

The future thought, that of tomorrow, will extend a serious challenge to mere faith. It will be a new age of rationalism, but not necessarily one of intolerant radicalism.

Like a light in the dark of a dismal night, let your self stand out as glowing, warm, and welcome.

It has been said that the only good is "The desire to do good." This is so because such a *good* is not expressed in the diverse terms of individual values.

Soul is not a thing. It is an experience; an experience for which man ever gropes for words to express it.

Rare knowledge, like gold, must be dug for, but in scholarly tomes, not soil!

Whenever morality is ineffective, conscience is inhibited, the right becomes only that which serves the personal self.

There is ever the struggle of the human mind to find its place in the whole of reality.

The *universality* of the *human will* is not found in just similar human actions; it is not what actions the will takes, but rather that it can *determine* its actions.

Whisperings of Self

We may not respect all the beliefs of others, but we should respect their right to have them.

All study reveals a personal vacuum, which knowledge alone can fill.

We may let imagery stimulate our thought, but we should not let it enmesh our reason in fantasy.

It is not what men believe that matters, but what actions emerge from their beliefs.

How can a man be free who does not think for himself? After all, it is only one who *thinks* who makes a true choice. All others are bound to the influence of suggestion, whether it be subtle or direct.

We are not chosen to be illuminated, we must *choose* to be illuminated.

The Unknown is the Undiscovered.

Education does not consist of the books read but rather the content that can be recalled.

The greatest of all *constants* is *change*.

Purpose sets forth certain ends, goals, or objectives to be attained. The human *will* becomes the motivating force by which they are attained. The *action* of will always represents our most dominant desire. *Purpose*, therefore, must rationally and emotionally arouse the *will* for the necessary motivation to attain the end sought.

Philosophy is the struggle to know.
Science is the *search* for knowledge.
Technology is the reduction of knowledge to application.
The first is the *intellectual* satisfaction.
The second is explorative *creativity*.
The third is the adaptation to *self* (social need).

Knowledge is like a rare gem—the more facets it has, the greater its brilliance.

Nothing worthwhile is attained easily. If it is, it is not fully appreciated because it has not a part of the self in it.

While there is life, there is hope. Life is the greatest gift we have. With life, we have that consciousness and the ability to realize the magnitude of the Cosmic.

When you are being copied, consider it an incentive to retain your lead.

Conscience imposes feelings of restraint on those actions that would disrupt the unity of self and the psychic.

The *self* comprises every state of *awareness* of which our being is capable.

The Infinite, the finite; from which comes the idea of the other? The nature of the Infinite cannot suggest the finite. An Infinite is boundless, there are no limits which can be perceived within it. Therefore, the notion of the finite cannot rise from the Infinite. However, what appears as finite implies the possibility of it expanding beyond itself. From the finiteness of his own being, man came to realize the infinity of the universe about him.

The more advanced and learned a society, the more complex and higher it is in the sense of being more all-embracing in its religious ideals. Consequently, the expression of spirituality of the individual, in some elements of society, may appear to be more lofty by comparison with a lower culture. But the inner, subjective impulse of response to what is felt as the spiritual motivation may be no greater in one culture or individual so inclined than in another.

Life is a drive, but you have to do the steering.

Spirituality is a personal belief being engendered, on the one hand by an innate sense of righteousness, and on the other hand by the belief in a transcendent infinite power of goodness.

Man cannot be an escapee from nature, but he likes to believe that there were mortals who were.

Mastership is recognized in action, that is, in *doing*. And this doing is noticeable because of its superiority or it is that action of which others are incapable. This mastership is not a faculty limited to certain individuals. It is not something which is bestowed upon someone. It may be potential in one, like an indwelling talent. Yet, until it is aroused or developed and *manifests* itself, it does not exhibit mastership.

All types of desires are a motivation for happiness of a kind. And such is the substance of *Love*.

He who professes to know the absolute Truth, is but knowing agreement with his own conclusions.

Curiosity is the challenge of the *unknown*. It is the undefined emotional response to physical and emotional stimuli.

The *soul* should be rationally thought to be beyond either corruption or perfection by man—the premise being that, since it is of a divine source, it lies beyond human power to alter in any manner its pristine nature.

For a thing to *be*, it must be innately in harmony with that of which it consists; and *consciousness* is that state of harmony.

Goals and fancies *motivate* the individual to *action*. Fancy may please, but it does not achieve.

Self is a unique phase of the stream of consciousness. It is the *consciousness of consciousness*. It is the awareness that we are apart from all else. More succinctly, it is consciousness looking back upon *itself*. *Self*-consciousness, thus, is the *highest* form of consciousness.

The *true* master of transcendent and mystical knowledge does not tend to portray himself as a personal guide of the lives of other mortals. He does not teach or imply that others must be *dependent* upon him. He does not advocate that they seek him out in meditation or personally whenever a problem arises. Simply, he does not want to create a dependency upon himself, for he knows that each human has his own *slumbering* master within to be awakened and brought to the threshold of consciousness. This slumbering master is the *whole* of self of which most men are but partly aware.

Consciousness, awareness, *cannot exist by itself.* Simply, you cannot be conscious without being *conscious of something.*

The power of a sacred place lies not in its form or tradition alone, but in the higher state of consciousness it can evoke in you.

Whisperings of Self

One who *continuously*, by whatever method, is seeking guidance from a Cosmic Master that has transcended this Earth, is *forfeiting* his own *personal mastership*. He is actually opposing the *true* purpose of those esoteric teachers, which is to provide us with the means of attaining our own personal mastership, *here and now.*

To follow the *ideals* and *teachings* of a truly enlightened being is one thing; but to desire only to be *led* by him is a *false* concept of mastership. For mastership, in any role, is *active*, never submissive.

Simplicity of accomplishment is indicative of personal mastership.

A thing or event cannot be a necessity in itself. It must be related to that which is *thought to require it.*

There are two universal concepts of the cosmos. One is that the cosmos is the result of a primary cause, and that it has an ultimate or final purpose.

The other concept postulates the cosmos as self-existent and having an all-inclusive oneness.

The first notion arises from attributing human-like qualities to the cosmos.

The second notion is more abstract; it endeavors to have the cosmos transcend any parallelism with human attributes.

Is the Greater Universe Both Finite and Infinite?

If the universe is the totality of all there is, then it is *finite* by the limiting quality of its own nature. The universe is also *infinite* because its nature has no beginning or end in *time*. The *space* of the universe is infinite because there is naught but its own nature to bound it. If the universe contracts and expands, then proportionately so does all else contained within it. Therefore, in either state, contraction or expansion, space would remain *relatively* the same.

Religion and Science

Religion is now a dependence upon supernatural powers to provide what at the moment is beyond human accomplishment. Religion has made the mistake of attempting to explain how a god acts. Human experience has too often proved such theories false.

To survive, religion must always represent an idealism yet to be attained. If religion shall keep its god an indeterminable cause which continually remains behind all that comes to the fore of human understanding, then it shall never be breached by any science or exposed as a misconception.

Man and his world are a series of causes and effects more infinite than the inquiries of the human mind. It is futile to define a first cause behind the whole, because the whole is its own cause. Unless the human mind can encompass the whole, it cannot presume to know the cause. The whole cause will ever remain supreme, never dethroned by discovery but exalted by it.

Make a man realize that the extent of the universe will ever exceed an expanding human intelligence, and you will inculcate within even the rankest materialist a religious reverence of existence.

Religion must take its god out of the realm of ideas and things, and make of him the inscrutable whole. Learning and knowledge can thus become reverend tools for building a religion which shall correspondingly grow with man's enlightenment.

About a Sheet of Paper

There is something so awesome about a crisp, white sheet of writing paper as it lies before you. It has a virtue of its own in its freshness and freedom from blemish. It dares you to alter its appearance with strange little characters, lines, and curlicues. As you look upon its unmarred surface, you feel as one gazing into a mirror. Anything may become reflected there. Out of its depths may arise great aspiration, towering ideals, images of glory that may move men's souls to nobler deeds, each word framed against the pearly background like a gem, and the whole a rare jewel.

But again, the labor completed, the marks are often but a hideous reminder of a spoiled material and a futile effort. At times one looks back upon the tracings before him wishing he had never advanced so far. Ahead of him is yet a great expanse of open, white smoothness. It has lost its appeal and has become but a taunt. To begin again is to wander back through a labyrinth of thoughts that mock your pride. As one poises his pen above the sheet, he feels not unlike a knight upon bold adventure. He hopes that upon his return the paper may fly from the masthead of his vanity and herald him as a craftsman of words and not a despoiler of the virginity of a white sheet of paper!

Whisperings of Self

My Friends

No man has a greater host of friends than I. Of an evening, some will take me on high adventure. Through icy blasts and over frozen regions we will journey. I will be numb with cold, and my eyes will ache from the unrelenting glare of sun on eternal white. Then again, on occasion, in torrid lands we will travel, each cutting and hacking his way through the green hell, as savage eyes peer out at us from the dismal darkness of the shadows.

Some of these companions of mine, of a night, will choose to leave the confines of this earth. With them I will vault into space. They stop at the moon, push their way through its moribund canyons, and thence they swirl and dance with the nebulae as I breathlessly keep pace. Never a night the same. Others of this host lead me into the past to silently witness sacred ceremonies of the ancients. We dine with Caesar. We fight in the legions of Alexander the Great, or we tarry awhile to listen to the deathless words of the sages who are gathered in the shadows of the Parthenon.

My life is ever a full one, for my friends are full of spirit. Their resourcefulness is the capacity of all human thought and endeavor. These friends are ever near. Their escapades, lives, and sentiments are just within the reach of my extended arm, for these friends are the treasured books upon my shelves. At attention they stand, a legion of personalities waiting to leap at my desire and serve my every mood and interest.

The soul of man is the site of his emotion,
Bearing the fruits of his thought,
And the story of his devotion;
A vast elevated plane, seared by the many fires
Of tempting pain,
Raising the mind to a lofty peak,
Where to troubled body it may speak
Of the soul divine and its glorious reign.

Life is a formation of ridges on the surface of time,
Whose valleys between are bridged with love
And held as a shrine.
The goal ever far distant but always in sight,
To be reached by the man whose footsteps are
guided
Not by the sword of might,
But by the true torch of endeavor and light.

—Ralph M. Lewis

1922 (age 18)

THE ROSICRUCIAN ORDER
Purpose and Work of the Order

Anticipating questions which may be asked by the readers of this book, the publishers take this opportunity to explain the purpose of this Order and how you may learn more about it.

There is only one universal Rosicrucian Order existing in the world today, united in its various jurisdictions, and having one Supreme Council in accordance with the original plan of the ancient Rosicrucian manifestoes. The Rosicrucian Order is not a religious or sectarian society.

This international organization retains the ancient traditions, teachings, principles, and practical helpfulness of the Order as founded centuries ago. It is known as the *Ancient Mystical Order Rosae Crucis,* which name, for popular use, is abbreviated into AMORC. The Headquarters of the Worldwide Jurisdiction (The Americas, Australasia, Europe, Africa, and Asia) is located at San Jose, California.

The Order is primarily a humanitarian movement, making for greater Health, Happiness, and Peace in people's *earthly lives,* for we are not concerned with any doctrine devoted to the interests of individuals living in an unknown, future state. The Work of Rosicrucians is to be done *here* and *now;* not that we have neither hope nor expectation of *another* life after this, but we *know* that the happiness of the future depends upon *what we do today for others* as well as for ourselves.

Secondly, our purposes are to enable men and women to live clean, normal, natural lives, as Nature intended, enjoying *all* the privileges of Nature, and all benefits and gifts equally with all of humanity; and to be *free* from the shackles of superstition, the limits of ignorance, and the sufferings of avoidable *Karma.*

The Work of the Order—using the word "work" in an official sense, consists of teaching, studying, and testing such Laws of God and Nature as make our Members Masters in the Holy Temple (the physical body), and Workers in the Divine Laboratory (Nature's domains). This is to enable our Members to render *more efficient help* to those who do not know, and who need or require help and assistance.

Therefore, the Order is a School, a College, a Fraternity, with a laboratory. The Members are students and workers. The graduates are unselfish servants of God to Humanity, efficiently educated, trained, and experienced, attuned with the mighty forces of the Cosmic or Divine Mind, and Masters of matter, space, and time. This makes them essentially Mystics, Adepts, and Magi—creators of their own destiny.

There are no other benefits or rights. All Members are pledged to give unselfish Service, without other hope or expectation of remuneration than to Evolve the Self and prepare for a *greater* Work.

The Rosicrucian Sanctum membership program offers a means of personal home study. Instructions are sent once a month in specially prepared weekly lectures and lessons, and contain a summary of the Rosicrucian principles with such a wealth of personal experiments, exercises, and tests as will make each Member highly proficient in the attainment of certain degrees of mastership. The lectures are under the direction of the Imperator's staff. These correspondence lessons and lectures comprise several Degrees. Each Degree has its own Initiation ritual, to be performed by the Member at home in his or her private home sanctum. Such rituals are not the elaborate rituals used in the Lodge Temples, but are simple and of practical benefit to the student.

If you are interested in knowing more of the history and present-day helpful offerings of the Rosicrucians, you may receive a *free* copy of the booklet entitled *The Mastery of Life*, by sending a request to:

Scribe W.O.S.
Rosicrucian Order, AMORC
Rosicrucian Park
San Jose, California 95191, U.S.A.

ROSICRUCIAN LIBRARY

ROSICRUCIAN QUESTIONS AND ANSWERS WITH COMPLETE HISTORY OF THE ORDER
by H. Spencer Lewis, F.R.C., Ph. D.

From ancient times to the present day, the history of the Rosicrucian Order is traced from its earliest traditional beginnings. Its historical facts are illuminated by stories of romance and mystery.

Hundreds of questions in this well-indexed volume are answered, dealing with the work, benefits, and purposes of the Order.

ROSICRUCIAN PRINCIPLES FOR THE HOME AND BUSINESS
by H. Spencer Lewis, F.R.C., Ph. D.

This volume contains the practical application of Rosicrucian teachings to such problems as: ill health, common ailments, how to increase one's income or promote business propositions. It shows not only what to do, but what to avoid, in using metaphysical and mystical principles in starting and bringing into realization new plans and ideas.

Both business organizations and business authorities have endorsed this book.

THE MYSTICAL LIFE OF JESUS
by H. Spencer Lewis, F.R.C., Ph. D.

A full account of Jesus' life, containing the story of his activities in the periods not mentioned in the Gospel accounts, *reveals the real Jesus* at last.

This book required a visit to Palestine and Egypt to secure verification of the strange facts found in Rosicrucian records. Its revelations, predating the discovery of the Dead Sea Scrolls, show aspects of the Essenes unavailable elsewhere.

This volume contains many mystical symbols (fully explained), photographs, and an unusual portrait of Jesus.

THE SECRET DOCTRINES OF JESUS

by H. Spencer Lewis, F.R.C., Ph. D.

Even though the sacred writings of the Bible have had their contents scrutinized, judged, and segments removed by twenty ecclesiastical councils since the year 328 A.D., there still remain buried in unexplained passages and parables the Great Master's *personal* doctrines.

Every thinking man and woman will find *hidden truths* in this book.

"UNTO THEE I GRANT..."

as revised by Sri Ramatherio

Out of the mysteries of the past comes this antique book that was written two thousand years ago, but was hidden in manuscript form from the eyes of the world and given only to the Initiates of the temples in Tibet to study privately.

It can be compared only with the writings attributed to Solomon in the Bible of today. It deals with man's passions, weaknesses, fortitudes, and hopes. Included is the story of the expedition into Tibet that secured the manuscript and the Grand Lama's permission to translate it.

A THOUSAND YEARS OF YESTERDAYS

by H. Spencer Lewis, F.R.C., Ph.D.

This fascinating story dramatically presents the real facts of reincarnation. It explains how the soul leaves the body and *when* and *why* it returns to Earth again.

This revelation of the *mystic laws and principles* of the Masters of the East has never before been presented in such a form. Finely bound and stamped in gold, it makes a fine addition to your library.

SELF MASTERY AND FATE WITH THE CYCLES OF LIFE

by H. Spencer Lewis, F.R.C., Ph. D.

This book demonstrates how to harmonize the self with the cyclic forces of each life.

Happiness, health, and prosperity are available for those who know the periods in their own life that enhance the success of varying activities. Eliminate "chance" and "luck," cast aside "fate," and replace these with self mastery. Complete with diagrams and lists of cycles.

ROSICRUCIAN MANUAL

by H. Spencer Lewis, F.R.C., Ph.D.

This practical book contains useful information that complements your Rosicrucian monograph studies. Included are extracts from the Constitution of the Rosicrucian Order, an outline and explanation of Rosicrucian customs, habits, and terminology, diagrams that illustrate important mystical principles, explanations of symbols used in the teachings, biographical sketches of AMORC officials, a glossary, and other helpful material. This book will answer many questions you may have about AMORC and its teachings, whether you are a Neophyte student or a member studying in the higher Degrees. The *Rosicrucian Manual* has been expanded and updated since its first printing to better serve our members through the years.

MYSTICS AT PRAYER

Compiled by Many Cihlar, F.R.C.

The first compilation of the famous prayers of the renowned mystics and adepts of all ages.

The book *Mystics at Prayer* explains in simple language the reason for prayer, how to pray, and the Cosmic laws involved. You come to learn the real efficacy of prayer and its full beauty dawns upon you. Whatever your religious beliefs, this book makes your prayers the application not of words, but of helpful, divine principles. You will learn the infinite power of prayer. Prayer is man's rightful heritage. It is the direct means of man's communion with the infinite force of divinity.

BEHOLD THE SIGN

by Ralph M. Lewis, F.R.C.

Unwrap the veil of mystery from the strange symbols inherited from antiquity. What were the *Sacred Traditions* said to be revealed to Moses? What were the discoveries of the Egyptian priesthood?

This book is fully illustrated with *age-old secret symbols* whose true meanings are often misunderstood. Even the mystical beginnings of the *secret signs* of many fraternal brotherhoods today are explained.

MANSIONS OF THE SOUL

by H. Spencer Lewis, F.R.C., Ph. D.

Reincarnation—the world's most disputed doctrine! What did Jesus mean when he referred to the "mansions in my Father's house"? This book demonstrates what Jesus and his immediate followers knew about the rebirth of the soul, as well as what has been taught by sacred works and scholarly authorities in all parts of the world.

Learn about the cycles of the soul's reincarnations and how you can become acquainted with your present self and your past lives.

LEMURIA—THE LOST CONTINENT OF THE PACIFIC

by Wishar S. Cervé

Where the Pacific now rolls in a majestic sweep for two thousand miles, there was once a vast continent known as Lemuria.

The scientific evidences of this lost race and its astounding civilization with the story of the descendants of the survivors present a cyclical viewpoint of rise and fall in the progress of civilization.

THE TECHNIQUE OF THE MASTER
or The Way of Cosmic Preparation
by Raymund Andrea, F.R.C.

A guide to inner unfoldment! The newest and simplest explanation for attaining the state of Cosmic Consciousness. To those who have felt the throb of a vital power within, and whose inner vision has at times glimpsed infinite peace and happiness, this book is offered. It converts the intangible whispers of self into forceful actions that bring real joys and accomplishments in life. It is a masterful work on psychic unfoldment.

THE SYMBOLIC PROPHECY OF
THE GREAT PYRAMID
by H. Spencer Lewis, F.R.C., Ph. D.

The world's greatest mystery and first wonder is the Great Pyramid. Its history, vast wisdom, and prophecies are all revealed in this beautifully bound and illustrated book. You will be amazed at the pyramid's scientific construction and at the secret knowledge of its mysterious builders.

THE TECHNIQUE OF THE DISCIPLE
by Raymund Andrea, F.R.C.

The Technique of the Disciple is a book containing a modern description of the ancient, esoteric path to spiritual Illumination, trod by the masters and avatars of yore. It has long been said that Christ left, as a great heritage to members of His secret council, a private method for guidance in life, which method has been preserved until today in the secret, occult, mystery schools.

Raymund Andrea, the author, reveals the method for attaining a greater life taught in these mystery schools, which perhaps parallels the secret instructions of Christ to members of his council. The book is informative, inspiring, and splendidly written. Paperback.

MENTAL POISONING
THOUGHTS THAT ENSLAVE MINDS
by H. Spencer Lewis, F.R.C., Ph. D.

Must humanity remain at the mercy of evil influences created in the minds of the vicious? Do poisoned thoughts find innocent victims? Use the knowledge this book fearlessly presents as an antidote for such superstitions and their influences.

There is no need to remain helpless even though evil thoughts of envy, hate, and jealousy are aimed to destroy your self-confidence and peace of mind.

GLANDS—THE MIRROR OF SELF
by Onslow H. Wilson, Ph.D., F.R.C.

You need not continue to be bound by those glandular characteristics of your life which do not please you. These influences, through the findings of science and the mystical principles of nature, may be adjusted. The first essential is that of the old adage, "Know Yourself." Have revealed to you the facts about the endocrine glands—know where they are located in your body and what mental and physical functions they control. The control of the glands can mean the control of your life. These facts, scientifically correct, with their mystical interpretation, are presented in simple, nontechnical language, which everyone can enjoy and profit by reading.

THE SANCTUARY OF SELF
by Ralph M. Lewis, F.R.C.

Are you living your life to your best advantage? Are you beset by a *conflict of desires?* Do you know that there are various *loves* and that some of them are dangerous drives?

Learn which of your feelings to discard as enslaving influences and which to retain as worthy incentives.

The author, Imperator of the Rosicrucian Order, brings to you from his years of experience, the practical aspects of mysticism.

SEPHER YEZIRAH—A BOOK ON CREATION
or The Jewish Metaphysics of Remote Antiquity

by Dr. Isidor Kalisch, Translator

The ancient basis for Kabalistic thought is revealed in this outstanding metaphysical essay concerning all creation. It explains the secret name of Jehovah.

Containing both the Hebrew and English texts, its 61 pages have been photolithographed from the 1877 edition. As an added convenience to students of Kabala, it contains a glossary of the original Hebraic words and terms.

SON OF THE SUN

by Savitri Devi

The amazing story of Akhnaton (Amenhotep IV), Pharaoh of Egypt, 1360 B.C. This is not just the fascinating story of one life—it is far more. It raises the curtain on man's emerging from superstition and idolatry. Against the tremendous opposition of a fanatical priesthood, Akhnaton brought about the world's first spiritual revolution. He was the first one to declare that there was a "sole God." In the words of Sir Flinders Petrie (*History of Egypt*): "Were it invented to satisfy our modern scientific conceptions, his religio-philosophy could not be logically improved upon at the present day."

This book contains over three hundred pages. It is handsomely printed, well bound, and stamped in gold.

THE CONSCIOUS INTERLUDE

by Ralph M. Lewis, F.R.C.

With clarity of expression and insightful penetration of thought, this original philosopher leads us to contemplate such subjects as: the Fourth Dimension, the Mysteries of Time and Space; the Illusions of Law and Order; and many others of similar import.

As you follow the author through the pages into broad universal concepts, your mind too will feel its release into an expanding consciousness.

ESSAYS OF A MODERN MYSTIC

by H. Spencer Lewis, F.R.C., Ph. D.

These private writings disclose the personal confidence and enlightenment that are born of *inner experience*. As a true mystic-philosopher, Dr. Lewis shares with his readers the results of contact with the Cosmic Intelligence residing within.

COSMIC MISSION FULFILLED

by Ralph M. Lewis, F.R.C.

This illustrated biography of Harvey Spencer Lewis, Imperator of the Ancient Mystical Order Rosae Crucis, was written in response to the requests of thousands of members who sought the key to this mystic-philosopher's life mission of rekindling the ancient flame of *Wisdom* in the Western world. We view his triumphs and tribulations from the viewpoint of those who knew him best.

Recognize, like him, that the present is our *moment in Eternity*; in it we fulfill our mission.

WHISPERINGS OF SELF

by Validivar

Wisdom, wit, and insight combine in these brief aphorisms that derive from the interpretation of Cosmic impulses received by Validivar, whose true name is Ralph M. Lewis, Imperator of the Rosicrucian Order.

These viewpoints of all areas of human experience make an attractive gift as well as a treasured possession of your own.

HERBALISM THROUGH THE AGES

by Ralph Whiteside Kerr, F.R.C.

The seemingly magical power of herbs endowed them with a divine essence to the mind of early man. Not only did they provide some of his earliest foods and become medicines for his illnesses but they also symbolized certain of his emotions and psychic feelings. This book presents the romantic history of herbs and their use even today.

ETERNAL FRUITS OF KNOWLEDGE

by Cecil A. Poole, F.R.C.

A stimulating presentation of philosophical insights that will provoke you into considering new aspects of such questions as: the purpose of human existence, the value of mysticism, and the true nature of good and evil. Paperback.

CARES THAT INFEST...

by Cecil A. Poole, F.R.C.

With a penetrating clarity, Cecil Poole presents us with the key to understanding our problems so that we may open wide the door and dismiss care from our lives. The author guides us on a search for *true value* so that, in the poet's words, "the night will be filled with music," as the *cares* "silently steal away."

MENTAL ALCHEMY
by Ralph M. Lewis, F.R.C.

We can transmute our problems to workable solutions through *mental alchemy*. While this process is neither easy nor instantaneously effective, eventually the serious person will be rewarded. Certain aspects of our lives *can* be altered to make them more compatible with our goals. Use this book to alter the direction of your life through proper thought and an understanding of practical mystical philosophy.

———

MESSAGES FROM THE CELESTIAL SANCTUM
by Raymond Bernard, F.R.C.

The real *unity* is Cosmic Unity. You are never separated from the Cosmic, no matter where you live or how different your lifestyle may be. Each person is like a channel through which cosmically inspired intuitive impressions and guidance can flow. This book explains how you can harmonize yourself with the *Celestial Sanctum*, an all-encompassing phenomenon that reveals rational, sensible, and practical messages of a cosmic nature. Allow this book to show you how your mind can become a window through which you can observe creation—and learn from it in a *personal way*.

———

IN SEARCH OF REALITY
by Cecil A. Poole, F.R.C.

This book unites metaphysics with mysticism. Man is not just an isolated entity on Earth. He is also of a great world—the Cosmos. The forces that create galaxies and island universes also flow through man's being. The human body and its vital phenomenon—Life—are of the same spectrum of energy of which all creation consists. The universe is you because you are one of its myriad forms of existence. Stripping away the mystery of this Cosmic relationship increases the personal reality of the Self. Paperback.

THROUGH THE MIND'S EYE

by Ralph M. Lewis, F.R.C.

Truth is what is real to us. Knowledge, experience, is the material of which truth consists. But what is the *real, the true,* of what we know? With expanding consciousness and knowledge, truth changes. Truth therefore is ever in the *balance*—never the same. But in turning to important challenging subjects, the *Mind's Eye* can extract that which is the true and the real, for the *now.* The book, *Through The Mind's Eye,* calls to attention important topics for judgment by your mind's eye.

———

MYSTICISM—THE ULTIMATE EXPERIENCE

by Cecil A. Poole, F.R.C.

An experience is more than just a sensation, a feeling. It is an *awareness,* or perception, with *meaning.* Our experiences are infinite in number, yet they are limited to certain types. Some are related to our objective senses; others, to dreams and inspirational ideas. But there is *one* that transcends them all—the *mystical experience.* It serves every category of our being: it stimulates, it enlightens, it strengthens; it is the *Ultimate Experience.*

And this book, *Mysticism—The Ultimate Experience,* defines it in simple and inspiring terms.

———

THE CONSCIENCE OF SCIENCE
and Other Essays

by Walter J. Albersheim, Sc.D., F.R.C.

A remarkable collection of fifty-four essays by one of the most forthright writers in the field of science and mysticism. His frank and outspoken manner will challenge readers to look again to their own inner light, as it were, to cope with the ponderous advances in modern technology.

THE UNIVERSE OF NUMBERS

From antiquity, the strangest of systems attempting to reveal the universe has been that of numbers. This book goes back to the mystical meaning and inherent virtue of numbers. It discusses the kabalistic writings contained in the *Sepher Yezirah,* and correlates the teachings of Pythagoras, Plato, Hermes Trismegistus, Philo, Plotinus, Boehme, Bacon, Fludd, and others who have explored this fascinating subject. *(Formerly published as "Number Systems and Correspondences.")* *Paperback.*

GREAT WOMEN INITIATES or The Feminine Mystic
by Hélène Bernard, F.R.C.

Throughout history, there have been women of exceptional courage and inspiration. Some, such as Joan of Arc, are well known; others have remained in relative obscurity—until now. In this book, Hélène Bernard examines from a Rosicrucian viewpoint the lives of thirteen great women mystics. Her research and insight have unveiled these unsung heroines who, even in the face of great adversity, have staunchly defended freedom of thought and the light of mysticism. Paperback.

INCREASE YOUR POWER OF CREATIVE THINKING IN EIGHT DAYS
by Ron Dalrymple, Ph.D., F.R.C.

Most people know they have the power within themselves to speak out and to do wonderful things, but they are constantly frustrated by not knowing how to get those great ideas out in the open. This new workbook contains simple but effective techniques designed to help you think more creatively. Its step-by-step program of exercises helps stimulate the flow of creative ideas by helping you develop a creative attitude and learn to think in creative patterns. Paperbound.

THE IMMORTALIZED WORDS OF THE PAST

Take a fascinating journey of the mind and spirit as you read these inspired writings. Fifty-eight of the world's most courageous thinkers bring you the benefit of their knowledge and experiences. Each excerpt is accompanied by a biographical sketch of its author. From Ptah-hotep to Albert Einstein, discover the wisdom of those who pioneered the highest avenues of human expression.

A SECRET MEETING IN ROME

by Raymond Bernard, F.R.C.

Experience a mystical quest for knowledge through this allegorical story of initiation. Narrated in the first person, this book symbolically explains the modern mission of the Order of the Temple and its connection with Atlantis, Pharaoh Akhnaton, and the Rose-Croix. You will also learn about the esoteric relationship between Christianity and Islam and the search for the Holy Grail. The author sheds light upon these mysteries and more as his dramatic story unfolds.